THE BEST CHRISTMAS

Unwrapping the Gift of Love

That Will Make this Your Best Christmas Ever

Suzanne Elizabeth Anderson

HENRY & GEORGE PRESS

Henry and George Press
Breckenridge, Colorado

Printed in the United States of America

First Printing, 2017

Henry and George Press
PO Box 7746
Breckenridge, CO 80424

www.suzanneelizabeths.com

by email: suzanne@suzanneelizabeths.com

Scripture quotations marked NIV are taken from the Holy Bible, New International Version, Copyright @1973

Scripture quotations marked MSG are taken from the Holy Bible, The Message, Eugene Peterson, Copyright @2016

Some material in this book previously appeared in the Summit Daily News in a faith column by Suzanne Elizabeth Anderson

CONTENTS

WEEK ONE:

Why did Jesus come into our world?

WEEK TWO:

Why should we make Jesus a daily part of our interior lives?

WEEK THREE:

Why should we live lives that allow people to see Jesus Christ in us?

WEEK FOUR:

Why do we need still need Jesus in our world today?

From this day forward…

Introduction

When do you put up your Christmas tree?

The answers on my Facebook page ranged from the day after Thanksgiving to December 25th. I put mine up last Monday. Mom informed me that hers went up on the same day.

The mantle above my fireplace is lined with elves, and bears, and nutcrackers. Around my Christmas tree are a bizarrely large collection of Santa Clauses. My small living room is festooned with every symbol of our cultural Christmas season.

Yet when you go upstairs, on a desk outside my bedroom you'll discover a hand-painted wooden egg from Ukraine depicting the Nativity, sitting at the base of an antique cross. Simple and profound.

The downstairs scene fills my nostalgic longing for the joy this season is meant to represent: a magical time with family and friends. The upstairs vignette is what is in my heart.

Exterior and interior. This season is heavy with meaning. Even those who do not believe in the Christ child, whose birth we celebrate, cling to the promise of loved ones gathered together to open gifts and share heartfelt warmth on one of the darkest nights of the year.

These two scenes: the colorful raucous holiday season of parties and shopping and eating, contrasted with the quiet solemnity of our anticipation of Jesus' birth, also describes our torn priorities.

Now we enter the season of Advent, four weeks preceding Christmas day. In the liturgical calendar, these weeks are meant to be a time of quiet preparation, as we ready ourselves to celebrate Jesus coming into the world as the Christ-child, Jesus in our lives each day, and Jesus' triumphant return in the Second Coming.

But how do we balance the external holiday demands of our lives with much-needed quiet meditation on the meaning of this season?

Traditionally, the four-candle Advent wreath is meant to focus our thoughts on one theme for each week: Hope and Forgiveness, Faith, Joy, and Justice and Peace. On Christmas Eve, a fifth candle is added to the center of the wreath to symbolize the birth of Jesus Christ.

But overarching the entire season of Advent, I'd like us to consider this question: Why?
Why did Jesus come into our world?
Why should we make Jesus a daily part of our interior lives?
Why should we live lives that allow people to see Jesus Christ in us?
Why do we need still need Jesus in our world today?

Over the next four weeks, we will consider each question and search for answers together.

Recently, I've been reading a book on the Biblical and historical life of Jesus, told through a pilgrimage to the Holy Land by a Jesuit priest. It reminded me of how much I take for granted in my knowledge of the birth and life of Jesus, and how little I actually know.

I believe we all fall into the trap of familiarity at this time of year. We've heard the Christmas story so many times, we forget why it is essential and how dramatically it changed the history of our world.

Which is why, I believe it's imperative that we reflect on the "Why" of the Christmas season. Advent is the perfect time ask ourselves why we believe in Jesus Christ, or, if we feel it's no longer necessary to believe?

Where do you fall on this continuum? Are you singing Christmas carols that announce the birth of the Newborn King with the same reverence as Frosty the Snowman?

The next four weeks of Advent are the perfect time to reflect on why we believe, or why we have lost our belief that Jesus can have a meaningful impact on our lives. Because if we can't see Jesus working in our lives, we are wasting our time in church each week.

When Jesus is alive in us, we are better for it and we share that love with others to make our world better. The next four weeks can change your life. Actually, God will change your life, are you ready?

Join me, please? Let's make this Season of Why culminate in our Best Christmas, ever.

WEEK ONE

Why did Jesus come into our world?

DAY 1

In the beginning God created the heavens and the
earth. [2] Now the earth was formless and
empty, darkness was over the surface of the
deep, and the Spirit of God was hovering over the
waters.

[3] And God said, "Let there be light," and there was
light. [4] God saw that the light was good, and he
separated the light from the darkness. [5] God
called the light "day," and the darkness he called
"night." And there was evening, and there was
morning—the first day.

Genesis 1:1-5 (NIV)

I suppose it's no coincidence that the Light of the World came into the world on one of the darkest nights of the year.

There is a lovely synchronicity that Jesus is called the Light of the World, a light that splits open the darkness separating history into two parts, before Christ and after Christ, just as God created light and separated the darkness to give us day and night.

When I was in my twenties, an enthusiastic young career woman working on Wall Street, one of the highlights of the year was waiting for Christmas lights and decorations to fill store windows along Fifth Avenue and Broadway, as well as the lighting of the Christmas tree in Rockefeller Center.

Crowds filled the sidewalks with people young and old who came to stare in wonder at the imaginative displays that made Christmas seem like a magical fairytale rather than the celebration of a Savior who came to Earth to save the world.

Yet, even within our beautifully decorated homes, despite the mounds of wrapped gifts piled beneath the twinkling Christmas tree, and the parties we attend where never a mention of the Baby Jesus is heard, we feel a longing in our hearts.

Something is missing.

When we leave the bright lights of the city's holiday decorations, or step outside our own homes into the night, we might suddenly feel an emptiness. Television commercials provide us with impossible standards of happy families who seem to have everything, every gift perfectly wrapped, every outfit neatly matched, every home perfectly calm.

But we know that it isn't always that way. Maybe not this year. A job has been lost, a child is sick, or an elderly-parent needs to move into our home. And suddenly, the high emotions of the holiday seem filled with more anxiety than joy.

As we stand outside in the darkness and stare up at the twinkling stars in the sky, we need a reminder of what this time of year can really mean to us.

DAY 2

[2-7] The people who walked in darkness
 have seen a great light.
For those who lived in a land of deep shadows—
 light! sunbursts of light!
You repopulated the nation,
 you expanded its joy.
Oh, they're so glad in your presence!
 Festival joy!
The joy of a great celebration,
 sharing rich gifts and warm greetings.
 For a child has been born—for us!
 the gift of a son—for us!
He'll take over
 the running of the world.
His names will be: Amazing Counselor,
 Strong God,
Eternal Father,
 Prince of Peace
His ruling authority will grow,
 and there'll be no limits to the wholeness he brings.
He'll rule from the historic David throne
 over that promised kingdom.
He'll put that kingdom on a firm footing
 and keep it going
With fair dealing and right living,
 beginning now and lasting always.
The zeal of God-of-the-Angel-Armies
 will do all this.
Isaiah 9:6-7(MSG)

"The people who walked in darkness have seen a great light". Hundreds of years passed from when that first promise was made, but it was always meant to be, never meant to be broken. Only waiting for the perfect circumstances.

The Light of the World came into our world and changed history forever. An infant born in a manger, a horse stable, to parents who were humble, ordinary, though Joseph could trace his lineage back to King David.

That juxtaposition perfectly captures how God chose to become man and enter the world as a vulnerable infant, no more protected from the harsh elements than any child born to humble circumstances back then, or today in many parts of the world. He cried when he was hungry, slept when he was tired, and looked up from his swaddling wrap into the eyes of his loving mother, Mary.

He would grow among members of his new family, becoming an inquisitive boy, a young man, and when he became a man, he finally grew into his ministry. It was then, as he traveled through his country, teaching and healing and creating miracles, he began to be recognized by the names foretold so many years ago:

Amazing Counselor, Strong God, Eternal Father, Prince of Peace

Although our calendar tells us there are still a few weeks to get done everything on our To-Do list, we can already feel the tension begin to creep into our shoulders.

There are cards to mail, awkward gifts to buy for the Secret Santa at work, or our child's teacher at school, people we hardly know more than as acquaintances. And then there are the latest toys for our children or the special gift wished by our spouse.

Sometimes we feel as if we are meant to be mind-readers to pick the gift that will bring a look of joy on Christmas morning rather than a look of disappointment. And if this wasn't enough, as the month moves forward we discover that the budget we promised to adhere to, is looking more and more unrealistic.

What we need more than ever is this One who is called the Amazing Counselor, the Prince of Peace. We need to stop and experience even a few minutes in prayerful silence, where we feel God's presence, and hear that quiet inner voice that assures us that we are loved, just as we are.

DAY 3

For it is by grace you have been saved, through faith—
and this is not from yourselves, it is the gift of God— not
by works, so that no one can boast.
Ephesians 2:8-9 (NIV)

Grace makes no sense. Why would God give us free and unmerited love that we are not only unworthy of, but could also never return in equal measure?

But these past few weeks, involving both my dog, Max's, death and a de-cluttering operation due to a move, have given me a better perspective on God's grace.

Needing to be rid of a lot of furniture, I posted everything to Freecycle, a site where, as its name suggests, everything is free. As I did, I was intrigued to find another side to Freecycle, where people could ask for something they hoped to receive. How logical, and yet, how strange and enticing.

I made a wish! On I posted that I would love a pair of used snowshoes, nothing fancy, just to walk with my two Newfoundland dogs through the woods this winter. I didn't expect a reply.

A few weeks later I got a reply from a woman named Julie, in a nearby town. She had a pair of snowshoes and wanted me to have them. As I picked them up, I couldn't miss the joy on Julie's face, which I am sure was reflected back to her in mine. We'd both benefited from an unexpected gift – one to give, and one to receive. When I took the snowshoes out of their carrying bag, I saw that they were Red Feathers, the exact brand I'd dreamed of.

What have used snowshoes and dying Newfoundland dogs taught me about grace? Well, the extra month with Max enabled me to trade grief for gratitude, to focus my remaining time with Max on my overwhelming love for him. Julie's generosity brought me sheer, undeserved joy. Weren't these both experiences of blessing and unmerited favor? In both cases I got the smallest glimpse of the love of God. My own heart might be wide open to love, but it is also limited by human-ness.

Imagine how much greater the depth of love that is available to us from God, who has no limitations!

When we experience unexpected love and joy, we gain insight into God's love for us. The grace we receive when he forgives our sin and promises to never remember it, only because we asked for forgiveness.

There is nothing we can do to earn the love God has for us. If we tried, we would surely fail. Who can be so good, so pure for more than a minute? I can't.

And that is where God's grace becomes our bridge – this path of love meant to bring us closer to God, who asks nothing in return.

It's easier for me to understand and accept how thoroughly I loved Max than to understand God's love for me, and yet Max wasn't perfect. When he sat up front, he put more than one small puncture in the upholstery of the car seat, and the front dashboard was the target of the infamous Newfie drool. But, I saw beyond all that to the joy in his eyes that only made me love him more, and without reservation.

Can I see myself as God sees me, with all the small and large punctures I have been responsible for? This person God created and loves, despite all of that, simply because she is his creation – and a facet of himself?

I am beginning to grasp the tiniest bit of why and how God loves me, and that means, finally, I am beginning to grasp the tiniest bit about grace.

DAY 4

[8] Then the man and his wife heard the sound of the Lord God as he was walking in the garden in the cool of the day, and they hid from the Lord God among the trees of the garden. [9] But the Lord God called to the man, "Where are you?"

[10] He answered, "I heard you in the garden, and I was afraid because I was naked; so, I hid."

[11] And he said, "Who told you that you were naked? Have you eaten from the tree that I commanded you not to eat from?"

[12] The man said, "The woman you put here with me—she gave me some fruit from the tree, and I ate it."

[13] Then the Lord God said to the woman, "What is this you have done?"

Genesis 3:8-13 (NIV)

After the Fall, God came to Adam and Eve in the garden.

Adam and Eve had chosen to do the one thing that God has asked them not to do. The knowledge that they had sought in their choice to eat of the tree of Good and Evil suddenly made them acutely aware of their nakedness.

Nakedness was not the sin. Awareness of good and evil created an awareness that their disobedience was. And so, they hid from God as he walked through the garden. They hid, not because they were ashamed of their God-created bodies, but because they were ashamed of what they had done and sought to hide themselves from God, as if when he couldn't see them, he wouldn't be able to see what they had done.

Of course, their awareness enabled God to see what they had done. Yet, God still pursued them. Not to punish them, but to ask why?

Yes, there will always be consequences to our actions, especially those that cause harm to ourselves or others. And we will have to accept those consequences.

Yet, God pursues us. And he does so because he loves us. Adam and Eve turned their backs on God. And yet, God pursued them. God is always seeking us, out of love, out of a desire to reconcile us to himself. This first act of forgiveness of Adam and Eve, is the same love and forgiveness that motivated God to send his son, Jesus Christ, to earth, not as a Messiah King to enslave us or rule over us. He came as one of us, to a working-class family, in a working-class neighborhood, raised as a carpenter.

He freely chose all of this, in order to better experience what it meant to be fully human, to understand daily struggles.

The entire Bible is a journey from that encounter in the garden, forward, of God's pursuit of each of us. Not to punish, but to heal. Because God loves us so dearly, he pursues us and eventually takes our form, human, to be with us, here on earth, as in Heaven.

The Christmas story is the culmination of that pursuit of God's love for us. And it is also just the beginning of the greatest love story of all time.

DAY 5

¹⁻⁵ A green Shoot will sprout from Jesse's stump,
   from his roots a budding Branch.
The life-giving Spirit of God will hover over him,
   the Spirit that brings wisdom and understanding,
The Spirit that gives direction and builds strength,
   the Spirit that instills knowledge and Fear-of-God.
Fear-of-God
   will be all his joy and delight.
He won't judge by appearances,
   won't decide on the basis of hearsay.
He'll judge the needy by what is right,
   render decisions on earth's poor with justice.
His words will bring everyone to awed attention.
   A mere breath from his lips will topple the wicked.
Each morning he'll pull on sturdy work clothes and boots,
   and build righteousness and faithfulness in the land.
Isaiah 11:1-5 (MSG)

This passage from Isaiah was meant to describe the Messiah King, a great warrior who would come to save Israel.

And yet, as we now know Jesus, it perfectly described not a king, but the Messiah who came as one of us, a simple man, who happened to be God.

And yet, the clues are here in this passage from Isaiah. The life-giving Spirit of God will hover over him, the Spirit that brings wisdom and understanding. The Spirit that gives direction and builds strength, the Spirit that instills knowledge and Fear-of-God."

Of course, we say that now, reading this passage with the benefit of hindsight. Of course, the Holy Spirit of God would hover over Jesus. As we know, by definition of the Holy Trinity, God, Jesus, and Holy Spirit are One. The Holy Spirit is as inseparable from Jesus as God is. Yet, there is a sweetness in this description. Because as well as being God-In-Man, Jesus was wholly human.

Before Jesus left this mortal plane, one of his most important gifts to his followers was to promise that he was not leaving us alone, but that he would leave us with a great Counselor, the Holy Spirit, our Counselor and Comforter.

So, it makes perfect sense that in this passage from Isaiah, that the Spirit of God is described as bringing wisdom and understanding, direction, strength building, and instills a knowledge and fear of God. Because that is exactly what the gift of the Spirit to us. The gift that Jesus gave us.

I hope we will learn to allow the Spirit of God to become an active part of our life, to be as Jesus intended, our Counselor.

3 In those days John the Baptist came, preaching in the
wilderness of Judea 2 and saying, "Repent, for the
kingdom of heaven has come near." 3 This is he who was
spoken of through the prophet Isaiah:
"A voice of one calling in the wilderness,
'Prepare the way for the Lord,
   make straight paths for him."
4 John's clothes were made of camel's hair, and he had a
leather belt around his waist. His food was locusts and
wild honey. 5 People went out to him from Jerusalem and
all Judea and the whole region of the Jordan.
6 Confessing their sins, they were baptized by him in the
Jordan River.
7 But when he saw many of the Pharisees and Sadducees
coming to where he was baptizing, he said to them: "You
brood of vipers! Who warned you to flee from the
coming wrath? 8 Produce fruit in keeping with
repentance. 9 And do not think you can say to yourselves,
'We have Abraham as our father.' I tell you that out of
these stones God can raise up children for Abraham.
10 The ax is already at the root of the trees, and every
tree that does not produce good fruit will be cut down and
thrown into the fire.
11 "I baptize you with[b] water for repentance. But after
me comes one who is more powerful than I, whose
sandals I am not worthy to carry. He will baptize you
with[c] the Holy Spirit and fire. 12 His winnowing fork is
in his hand, and he will clear his threshing floor,
gathering his wheat into the barn and burning up the chaff
with unquenchable fire."
 Matthew 3:1-12 (NIV)

The four Gospels of the Bible portray different versions of Jesus. Matthew's gospel reads like a quickly drawn outline, a first draft Jesus. Mark presents the Rabbinical Jesus. Luke gives us a Jesus that shares so many of our traits, we can believe that he truly became human during his brief time on Earth. And then there is my favorite, the gospel of John, metaphysical, spiritual, intellectual Jesus. The mystic who speaks in parables that are so nuanced and filled with knowing that two thousand years later we still do not understand them all.

But who is my Jesus?

I am an amateur baker. Which is a nice way of saying that I'm basically a one-trick pony with an occasional flourish of rosemary and olives. While I don't know enough to produce loaves that match the ardor of my appetite, I've learned a few things from my mistakes.

Between the first rise and the moment the dough goes into the oven, there is moment when my efforts to shape the dough to my liking, by pulling it into a baguette or tucking it into a boule, will damage the dough's elasticity and it will no longer resemble what it was meant to be. What I end up with is no longer bread.

I believe I face the same danger in my relationship with Jesus.

When I look out on the landscape of the many descriptions of Jesus, it feels like we want to mold him into a someone who fits our needs or aspirations. When we are sick, we summon Dr. Jesus. When we run out of money, we call on Banker Jesus. Perhaps each version reflects the Jesus we need, an ever-changing reflection of our better selves. But of course, there is only one Jesus, and our limited vision allows us only a sliver of his true enormity.

I understand that Jesus became human so that we could experience a personal relationship and communion that could only be possible if we saw human-ness in him and believed that he understood our frailty.

Yet, I worry that when I see Jesus only as a provider of stuff, or a friend to pal around with, or more uncomfortably a spiritual-lover, I diminish the true sacred mystery that is due the Son of God.

When I was in college, during the Regan Era, my parents attended a conservative church where Jesus was a very stern Republican who conveyed a litany of things we should not do and people we should not associate with.

In the era of Pope Francis, Jesus seems more concerned that we love one another and care for those who are poor, displaced, and suffering.

Jesus speaks differently to millennial hipsters in a storefront church in Brooklyn, where they share the communion meal around a table and pass broken bread after they have blessed it and shared an informal homily.

Those words would probably sound strange to my 50-something Catholic ears that understand Jesus best through the formality of Eucharist.

The conservative church that my mother returned to, after living with me for twenty years, has changed. The 150-member robed choir is gone and so are the traditional hymns. In their place is a rock band that leads the congregation in contemporary choruses.

But it's also changed in a more important way: it has become a church that serves its community, its elderly, its homeless, as well as the young families that are now its majority.
Other than complaining to the new pastor that the band's drummer is too enthusiastic, my mother is very content there.

Of course, she is 90-years old and world-traveled. She has read her Bible and sat in prayer every day for decades, and she knows a Jesus that I cannot even imagine.

To be honest, I never gave Jesus careful consideration until recently. Yes, I accepted Jesus as my Savior and Lord. But I did not have a personal relationship with him. Although I knew that Jesus died and rose from the dead for my sins, I had not experienced his real loving presence.

Sometimes praying with Jesus feels like speaking into the wind. On a spiritual level, I understand that he is there. But on an emotional level, I am never sure that he is listening. I want to have a deep relationship with Jesus, to know that I am in his presence.

There are many moments when I am brought to tears of gratitude as I share communion during Mass. And though I am unable to experience his presence in prayer, I do not doubt his existence, or my love for him. This probably sounds like a strange confession for someone who writes a weekly faith column: Still, sometimes Jesus feels distant. I love him, but how can I experience his love for me?

WEEK TWO

Why should we make Jesus
a daily part of our interior lives?

DAY 7

6-10 We, of course, have plenty of wisdom to pass on to you once you get your feet on firm spiritual ground, but it's not popular wisdom, the fashionable wisdom of high-priced experts that will be out-of-date in a year or so. God's wisdom is something mysterious that goes deep into the interior of his purposes. You don't find it lying around on the surface. It's not the latest message, but more like the oldest—what God determined as the way to bring out his best in us, long before we ever arrived on the scene. The experts of our day haven't a clue about what this eternal plan is. If they had, they wouldn't have killed the Master of the God-designed life on a cross. That's why we have this Scripture text:

No one's ever seen or heard anything like this,
Never so much as imagined anything quite like it—
What God has arranged for those who love him.

But you've seen and heard it because God by his Spirit has brought it all out into the open before you.

10-13 The Spirit, not content to flit around on the surface, dives into the depths of God, and brings out what God planned all along. Whoever knows what you're thinking and planning except you yourself? The same with God—except that he not only knows what he's thinking, but he lets us in on it. God offers a full report on the gifts of life and salvation that he is giving us. We don't have to rely on the world's guesses and opinions. We didn't learn this by reading books or going to school; we learned it from God, who taught us person-to-person through Jesus, and we're passing it on to you in the same firsthand, personal way. 1 Corinthians 2:8-13 (MSG)

Although it was only 6:45 p.m., it felt much later. The snowstorm and plummeting temperatures had sent everyone inside. French Street was snow packed and empty as we crossed. Except for the lighted entrance ahead.

I felt a giddy sense of relief as I entered the warmly lighted sanctuary of St. Mary's and saw that the church was nearly full for the Wednesday evening Vigil Mass for the Immaculate Conception of Mary.

Earlier in the day, I'd had the following phone conversation with Mom, who is my first reader.

Me: "I want to write about joy this week, but I'm not feeling very joyful."

Mom: "Take the afternoon off, pour yourself a glass of wine, read, pray, it will come."

Since it was only noon, I made myself a pot of herbal tea, but otherwise followed Mom's advice. And at 7pm I joined my friend and her family at Mass, still with no idea of how I would write this week's column.

After receiving Communion, I knelt in my pew and asked God how I could write about joy when I wasn't feeling joyful. He replied, 'When do you feel joyful?'

That's when the light broke through. I realized the feeling I experienced as I entered the church was joy. And the feeling I experienced every time I received Communion was joy.

This church and this sacrament of Communion that I shared at least once a week was my source of joy.

On Facebook, this morning I saw a clever video that formed a Christmas tree from the many names of God. One of those names was Light of the World.

And that is exactly what I experienced last night as I crossed French Street and saw the welcoming lighted entrance of St. Mary's. Jesus, Immanuel, God with us, Holy Spirit, my Joy Forever.

Jesus' birth on a lonely night in the humblest of circumstances was the crack in history that let the light of love and joy and salvation come flooding into an otherwise dark and lost world.

He was light that sparked the stars that guided three wise men to kneel and worship by his side.

Jesus' arrival was the fulfillment of the psalm that promises, "weeping may last for the night, but rejoicing comes in the morning." (Psalm 30:5)

Life is unpredictable. When I looked for sources of joy earlier in the day, it was based on a scale of emotional and material things.

What I realized at the Vigil Mass on Wednesday night is my surest sense of joy will always come from God, from the fellowship I receive in his church, and always from Communion, that forever enduring sacrament of his love for us.

What I experienced in that moment after Communion, is something I believe I will remember for the rest of my life. When we seek joy from relationships or things, our experience of joy will be pleasing but fleeting. That's simply life.

When we open our hearts to God, we understand that He is our reliable and permanent source of joy. He will always be there for us. Always available, always limitless in love and understanding.

Like any relationship, we build our relationship with God through daily communication. We spend time with God in prayer, by reading the Bible, by seeking his will for our lives before our own will. Through consistent attention to God we discover a beautiful and loving relationship that will last the rest of our lives and beyond.

God loves us more than we can ever imagine. Through his son Jesus, he is the Light of the World and our Joy. He is our Morning Star, that guides us even today, to the infant in the manger. Our Newborn King.

DAY 8

[31-39] So, what do you think? With God on our side like this, how can we lose? If God didn't hesitate to put everything on the line for us, embracing our condition and exposing himself to the worst by sending his own Son, is there anything else he wouldn't gladly and freely do for us? And who would dare tangle with God by messing with one of God's chosen? Who would dare even to point a finger? The One who died for us—who was raised to life for us! —is in the presence of God at this very moment sticking up for us. Do you think anyone is going to be able to drive a wedge between us and Christ's love for us? There is no way! Not trouble, not hard times, not hatred, not hunger, not homelessness, not bullying threats, not backstabbing, not even the worst sins listed in Scripture:

They kill us in cold blood because they hate you. We're sitting ducks; they pick us off one by one.

None of this fazes us because Jesus loves us. I'm absolutely convinced that nothing—nothing living or dead, angelic or demonic, today or tomorrow, high or low, thinkable or unthinkable—absolutely nothing can get between us and God's love because of the way that Jesus our Master has embraced us.

Romans 8:31-39 (MSG)

When we think of God, if we think of Him at all, he seems very removed from our lives.

How could he ever appreciate what it feels like to lose a much-needed job and then worry about keeping our home and affording groceries? How would God know how it feels when we take our child to the doctor and the diagnosis isn't the flu, but leukemia?

Still, we send up prayers to this remote God. Even when they feel as effective as letting go of a balloon and watching it drift away on the random currents of the wind.

When the people of the Old Testament watched for the promised Messiah, they imagined he would "reign on David's throne and over his kingdom, establishing and upholding it with justice and righteousness from that time on and forever." (Isaiah 9:7)

Instead, our Messiah was born in a stable, a child of average parents. Yet with these humble beginnings, he fulfilled the first prophesy and first inkling of his destiny. "The virgin will conceive and give birth to a son, and they will call him Immanuel" (which means "God with us"). (Isaiah 7:14, Matthew 1:23)

As he grew into a man, a humble carpenter, he did not become a warrior like David, nor did he ever become a king. No wonder he was not accepted then or even now.

In the time of Jesus, as today, we live in war-torn countries where people are persecuted for what they believe, and where income disparity means that the cyclical dips in the economy can mean disaster for some and opportunity for others.

We live in a world where seemingly random life-taking acts of terror or crime or illness can create holes in a heart that leave us doubled over in stunned shock, no matter what our economic status.

Can the people of the Old Testament, or we today, be blamed for imagining that our Savior could only come to save us as an invincible warrior king?

Yet, inexplicably, God had a much more radical idea of what "God with us" would mean.

Had Jesus Christ fulfilled the wishes of his people by taking the mantle of warrior king, he could easily have restored the freedom and fortunes of the people of Israel. And certainly, that would have fulfilled God's promise to His chosen people.

Instead, God had a greater plan. He came not to save and restore one group, but all people.

Had Jesus come as a king to unite the entire world under one banner, he would have been removed from us. After all, when is the last time that a commoner sat down to dinner with a king?

How could a king understand the needs of a blind man, the sorrows of a prostitute, the insecurities and jealousy of two sisters?

Such simple, essential humanity would never be experienced by a Messiah King.

Which is why God, in His infinite wisdom, not only became human, he lived among us as a common man. He experienced our tears of sorrow when a child died in our arms. He laughed with us around a wedding table where we drank wine. He understood and forgave a best friend who made a promise he could not keep.

Yes, Jesus is best known for the miracles he performed, but it was his daily involvement in our lives that allows us to claim, "God with us."

Even as he was crucified, nailed through hands and legs to a cross, left to die in agony, experiencing the very human feeling of abandonment as he cried out, "My God, why have you forsaken me?"

I never understood this moment between Father and Son.

Until I realized that "God with us" means always with us, even in the darkest hour. Even when we cry out in agony and hear no reply. God is still with us.

It is only when "God with us" has experienced every aspect of our humanity, our broken body, our broken heart, that the resurrection can convey the love, forgiveness, and redemption encompassed in one life.

Jesus chose to be "God with us" rather than a warrior king removed from us. Because he chose to save all of us rather than some of us, he has been rejected by most of us.

We wanted a Messiah who would ride into battle with us, kill our enemies and show our superiority by exerting his overwhelming power.

Instead, we received a Messiah who taught us to love our enemies, to feed the poor, to include all people in the gift of God's love.

Because he lived as a humble man, he was called a prophet, a teacher, a rabbi, only human.

But when we examine his life and his legacy, we can conclude that he is "God with us", the personification of God's desire to experience our humanity and demonstrate his love for us by sharing our lives.

So that when we pray, we can know that he has been here too.

DAY 9

[14] The Word became flesh and blood,
   and moved into the neighborhood.
We saw the glory with our own eyes,
   the one-of-a-kind glory,
   like Father, like Son,
Generous inside and out,
   true from start to finish.

John 1:14 (MSG)

How can I possibly give glory to the One who possesses all glory?

Then he was told, "Go, stand on the mountain at attention before God. God will pass by." A hurricane wind ripped through the mountains and shattered the rocks before God, but God wasn't to be found in the wind; after the wind an earthquake, but God wasn't in the earthquake; and after the earthquake fire, but God wasn't in the fire; and after the fire a gentle and quiet whisper. (1 Kings 19:11)

When I consider what it must be like to experience God's glory, this scripture passage is what I hope for. It speaks to God's gentle love for us, his intention that we never be given more than we can handle, and his wish for communion with us, on a deeply personal level.

A few weeks ago, as I sat in church during my evening hour of Adoration, I was silently talking to God about my work. First, I asked, why does God care so much that we work to become our best selves?

And the thought came that we do so to make *THIS* world better. Then I asked God what he could possibly receive from our best efforts. And the thought came that our purpose is to give God glory. But how can *I* possibly give glory to God, who possesses all glory? This is part of the great mystery.

At Mass, we sing within the text of the Gloria: "Almighty God and Father, we worship You, we give You thanks, we praise You for Your glory."

We sing the words every week, but do we stop to think what this means for our daily lives? St. Paul expressed it with this all-encompassing statement: "Whatever you do, do all to the glory of God". (1 Corinthians 10:31)

If we take St. Paul's direction seriously, it sets an important new standard for the choices we make each day.

If we consciously attempt to live our best lives to glorify God, then everything we do reflects our love for God, so that others see God in us and become attracted; they want to experience God in their own lives. Our actions, then, become acts of thanksgiving, gratitude, and praise for God's greatness and for his love.

How do we live our best lives? By understanding our frailties, counting on God's mercy, and trying each day to use the gifts God has given to us, freely — gifts that, Pope Francis reminds us, are never taken away:

"…there will be sins, there will be disobedience, but in the face of this disobedience there is always mercy. It is like the dynamic of our walking, journeying toward maturity: there is always mercy, because He is faithful, He never revokes His gifts. It is linked; this is linked, that the gifts are irrevocable; [but] why? Because in the face of our weaknesses, our sins, there is always mercy. And when Paul comes to this reflection, he goes one step further: but not in explanation for us, but of adoration." In Adoration, we worship, and we meditate, but what does it mean to give God the glory?

Thanks, and praise, humility and awe, certainly. But what God wants most is our *LOVE*. We were created by God out of love. He sent his son, Jesus, to become human and live with us because he loved us so dearly. God seeks to brings us close to him, because he loves us.

It is only natural to conclude that what God wants most from us is to see that love returned freely and joyfully — through our obedience, through the joyful use of the gifts he has given us to help us live our lives to the fullest. "I came so that they might have life and have it more abundantly," said Jesus (John 10:10).

Imagine a mirror pointed at the sun, reflecting its light back to itself. In living our lives to the full, or at least honestly trying to, we become mirrors reflecting God's love for us, back to him. We show him our love in that powerful way: light unto Light. And then, of course, in our joy and our peace, we show that Light to the world.

What do you give someone who has everything? Love is a wonderful place to start. Even if that someone is God.

To be honest, my understanding is a work in progress, but this is a good place to begin: With a heart filled with gratitude, I give all honor and praise and glory to God through the very gifts he has given me, and I love him with all my heart.

DAY 10

³⁹⁻⁴⁵ Mary didn't waste a minute. She got up and traveled to a town in Judah in the hill country, straight to Zachariah's house, and greeted Elizabeth. When Elizabeth heard Mary's greeting, the baby in her womb leaped. She was filled with the Holy Spirit, and sang out exuberantly,

You're so blessed among women,
and the babe in your womb, also blessed!
And why am I so blessed that
the mother of my Lord visits me?
The moment the sound of your
greeting entered my ears,
The babe in my womb
skipped like a lamb for sheer joy.
Blessed woman, who believed what God said,
believed every word would come true!
Luke 2:39-45 (MSG)

I joined the Catholic Church 30 years ago as an adult. Although I've often said that Mary brought me into the Church, quite honestly (having been raised in a Protestant tradition) I often struggled with how I should relate to Our Lady. For years, I thought of her as distant, the image described in Revelation, a queenly figured wearing a crown surrounded by stars, standing on a globe with the "serpent" crushed beneath her feet. "Hail, Holy Queen!"

And then there was the Rosary, "Mary's Crown" – the stumbling block for so many newcomers and cradle Catholics alike.

To be honest, my mind often wandered as I tried to say an entire Rosary. Which is why after reading an article about a Living Rosary — where a group of people commit to saying just one decade of a Rosary per day — I was inspired to form such a group within my church. My hope was that over the course of 20 weeks I would form the habit of saying the Rosary each day and begin to understand what drew people to the prayer — people who encountered it as something they looked forward too, rather than a chore.

I'm sorry to say that I failed to meet even this small daily goal more times than I succeeded, and I frankly still didn't understand the devotion felt by others.

So, I felt a like a fraud when an interviewer asked how the Living Rosary had changed my relationship with Mary. I blurted out, "Saying the Rosary humanized Mary for me. It made me understand that she is a model of how we should live in relationship to God!"

Where did that come from? I'd never consciously had that thought before. Yet, once I said it out loud it made perfect sense. During the weeks of saying the Rosary, I realized that each of the 20 mysteries is a Scripture-based event from the life of Jesus, from the visitation Mary first receives to Jesus' death and resurrection. The Rosary points to the Bible, because it's based on events from the Bible.

As I thought about this, I imagined one of the first scenes in which we encounter Mary, as portrayed in the First Joyful Mystery, when the Angel Gabriel appears and greets Mary saying, "Hail, full of grace, the Lord is with thee: blessed art thou among women." (Luke 1:28)

Mary's response, ultimately, is "Behold the handmaid of the Lord; be it done to me according to thy word." And this is where I finally began to understand: God has given Mary a unique purpose for her life, but never against her will. She is being asked to step out into the unknown, to accept that God's plan for her life is better than anything she could accomplish on her own.

We are also asked by God to accept that he has a unique plan for our lives that first requires our trust.

After Jesus is born, we catch glimpses of Mary relating to Jesus as a mother relates to her child. I smile every time I think about Mary asking Jesus to turn the water into wine. This helped me to understand that God seeks an intimate, familial relationship with each of us. He wants us to come to him each day with our hopes, our grievances, our sorrow, and even our most ordinary requests.

Mary's love for Jesus allows her to follow him all the way to the end, to stand at the foot of the cross as he is crucified. She demonstrates the trust to remain firm in our commitment to God even in our darkest hour, when all hope is lost.

Mary's loyalty is rewarded by Jesus' consolation when he says to one of his disciples, "Behold, your mother," and to Mary, "Behold, your son." Just as Mary is never left abandoned by Jesus, so we also will never be deserted in our desolation.

I now understand Mary as a godly woman I want to emulate. I want to surrender to God's better plan for my life. I want to include God in every area of my life. I want to love God until the end of my life, when my heart is broken and when Jesus fills it with joy.

Having never quite "gotten" the meaning of "To Jesus through Mary," I now look forward to saying the Rosary with this new understanding of Our Lady — the preeminent model of how we are called to a deeper relationship with God.

DAY 11

[5-8] Think of yourselves the way Christ Jesus thought of himself. He had equal status with God but didn't think so much of himself that he had to cling to the advantages of that status no matter what. Not at all. When the time came, he set aside the privileges of deity and took on the status of a slave, became human! Having become human, he stayed human. It was an incredibly humbling process. He didn't claim special privileges. Instead, he lived a selfless, obedient life and then died a selfless, obedient death—and the worst kind of death at that—a crucifixion.

[9-11] Because of that obedience, God lifted him high and honored him far beyond anyone or anything, ever, so that all created beings in heaven and on earth—even those long ago dead and buried—will bow in worship before this Jesus Christ, and call out in praise that he is the Master of all, to the glorious honor of God the Father.

Philippians 2:5-11 (MSG)

Years ago, I briefly belonged to a church where we were judged by the clique we belonged to within the congregation, the quality of the clothes we wore, or the amount of money in our bank account. Although I am certain everyone in the church loved God. I often had the feeling that there were some who felt that they were closer to God because they were closer to the pastor or his wife's social circle.

And perhaps that is why the Christian church has split into so many disparate directions over the past two thousand years. What began as a straightforward ministry based on two simple but profound commandments: that we should love God, and love one another as we love ourselves.

And that we should accept that God became man to shed his blood for us, to forgive our sins. Became a place so tangled with rules and power struggles and the best and worst parts of humanity. And now we have hundreds of denominations, and churches being held in nightclubs and cathedrals, singing hymns in Latin and those accompanies by rock bands.

And through all these machinations, do we forget Jesus? Or do these things help us to see him more clearly? I believe we must all find our 'church' where we can see Jesus most clearly. John the Baptist, preaching in the wilderness. Saint Francis and his gentle vow of poverty. The history changing work of Pope John Paul II from a most ornate cathedral in Rome. The work of Mother Teresa in garbage strewn streets of India. We will find Jesus in all these places.

Wherever we are, I hope Jesus does not become lost in a church that tries to conform to the world, rather than asking the world to make room for Jesus. I hope we never forget that Jesus is not just a preacher or prophet, he is the Son of God.

As I was driving to the post office the other morning, I was thinking about this and in my mind's eye, I saw myself standing in the yard of a house, an elderly man handed me keys to the front door, hugged me and said, "God has not forgotten you."

It was a passing moment, a waking fantasy except for the old man's message. Because the truth is that I have felt forgotten by God. And so, I held onto that sentence like a prayer.

When that is all we have, that is what we must do and then we must surrender the prayer to God.

After we have given thanks, given of ourselves, given our talents and treasures, the final and most difficult thing we release to God is the burden of worry that we clutch to our hearts.

When we have given all of that to God, our hearts and hands are open to receive His goodness, His blessing, but most importantly the gift that can heal us and make us whole.

The meaning of Advent is twofold: We celebrate the beginning of the hope we received when God joined us as a fragile babe, became man, and taught us the meaning of love so big it could not be contained by this world. And then, we celebrate the anticipation of His return.

The difference between my dark ruminations of past failures and future worries, and Advent's celebration of the past and anticipation of the future is that God's way is filled with hope. God has not forgotten us. Let's not forget God this Christmas.

DAY 12

⁹⁻¹⁶ I'm single-minded in pursuit of you;
   don't let me miss the road signs you've posted.
I've banked your promises in the vault of my heart
   so I won't sin myself bankrupt.
Be blessed, God;
   train me in your ways of wise living.
I'll transfer to my lips
   all the counsel that comes from your mouth;
I delight far more in what you tell me about living
   than in gathering a pile of riches.
I ponder every morsel of wisdom from you,
   I attentively watch how you've done it.
I relish everything you've told me of life,
   I won't forget a word of it.
¹⁷⁻²⁴ Be generous with me and I'll live a full life;
   not for a minute will I take my eyes off your road.
Open my eyes so I can see
   what you show me of your miracle-wonders.
I'm a stranger in these parts;
   give me clear directions.
My soul is starved and hungry, ravenous!—
   insatiable for your nourishing commands.
 Yes, your sayings on life are what give me delight;
   I listen to them as to good neighbors!
Psalm 119:9-24 (MSG)

One night, I roll over in bed and pray, "Dear God, what should I write about?" In the morning, I take Henry and Max, my two Newfoundland dogs, for their morning walk. Again, I ask, "Dear God, what should I write about?"

And within my heart, I hear a whisper, "Why do you love me?" Immediately I want to brush the question aside. Surely there is something broader, less intimate than writing about *that*.

From the moment, I attend my first Sunday school class as a child, I learn Jesus loves me, proof in the words of the familiar song:

Jesus loves me this I know
For the Bible tells me so
Little ones to him belong
They are weak, but he is strong
Yes, Jesus loves me
Oh, yes Jesus loves me
Yes, Jesus loves me for the Bible tells me so

And so, I accept that Jesus loves me. And I agree without a second thought, that I love Jesus, too. But how often do I ask myself *why* I love Jesus? I find it uncomfortable. Not in a religious obligation way, nor because I learned to, but in a personal way. *Why do you, Suzanne Elizabeth Anderson, love me?*

Dear Jesus,

Is it because when you feed five thousand, you teach me that service and kindness multiply as we give them away? Maybe I love you, Jesus because you give me a message of love when I feel poor, sick, and discarded.

You never ridicule my suffering or shortcomings. You hold my face in your hands, look me in the eye, and tell me I can begin again. Maybe it is because you are the giver of second chances.

At the Last Supper, you predict Peter will deny you three times. Peter, your most loyal disciple, replies this is impossible. Still, Peter does deny you three times before dawn. After your resurrection, you not only forgive Peter, you redeem him.

Then, Jesus, you ask Peter three times if he loves you still, and after each question, Peter replies, 'you know I love you.' And then Jesus, you command him, 'go and feed my sheep,' taking Peter's brokenness and using it to build your church.

I love you, Jesus, because you sacrifice your life for my sins even though you know I will deny you and turn away. I am Peter. Redeemed when my love for you falls short.

I love you, Jesus, because you love me when I cannot love myself. You run toward me on a dusty road, with arms wide open when I return as the prodigal daughter covered in filth and the weight of unspeakable things I have done to be loved. Jesus, you cover me with magnificent tapestry robes and hold a feast as if I return with honor when in fact I come back with nothing more than failure and shame. I love you, Jesus, because your infinite patience never shows me how far I must go, only how far I have come. Daily, you encourage me to become the woman you created me to be.

Because when I don't know myself, Jesus, you promise me that you knew me and loved me, 'before I was knit together in my mother's womb.' Because when I only see my ugliness, you tell me I am 'fearfully and wonderfully made.'

I love you, Jesus, because when I say, 'I cannot', you only ask that I say, 'yes'. And then you show me that "nothing is impossible with God."

I love you, Jesus, because you became human so you could tell me you remember how it feels when tears burn my exhausted eyes or become the overflow of my joy in you.

When I consider how little I comprehend, I love you, Jesus, because I will gladly spend the rest of my life sitting at your feet, knowing that if I study forever, I will only scratch the surface of your depthless mystery.

I love you, Jesus, because I will never understand how much you loved me, first.

DAY 13

$^{26-28}$ Meanwhile, the moment we get tired in the waiting, God's Spirit is right alongside helping us along. If we don't know how or what to pray, it doesn't matter. He does our praying in and for us, making prayer out of our wordless sighs, our aching groans. He knows us far better than we know ourselves, knows our pregnant condition, and keeps us present before God. That's why we can be so sure that every detail in our lives of love for God is worked into something good.

$^{29-30}$ God knew what he was doing from the very beginning. He decided from the outset to shape the lives of those who love him along the same lines as the life of his Son. The Son stands first in the line of humanity he restored. We see the original and intended shape of our lives there in him. After God made that decision of what his children should be like, he followed it up by calling people by name. After he called them by name, he set them on a solid basis with himself. And then, after getting them established, he stayed with them to the end, gloriously completing what he had begun.

Romans 8:28-30 (MSG)

When Jesus left, he promised that we would not be left alone, but that he would send the Holy Spirit, the Spirit of God, to be with us, to be our counselor. But what is it like to be in the presence of the Holy Spirit?

If you walk into my parish church on any given Thursday between 5 and 6 p.m. you might be confused. In the dim light of early evening, you will find four to 20 people sitting in silence, at a polite distance from one another, heads bowed, or gazing at the altar. Some might even be reading.

You could think they were waiting for something to happen. The start of a church service, perhaps?

But, no, not at this time.

Instead, each person will sit for the entire hour in silence. And yes, you will see a core group of the same people every week. I've become one of them. Apart from Mass, this is the hour I look forward to most each week.

In our weekly church bulletin, it's listed simply as "Adoration." It's also known as Adoration of the Blessed Sacrament, an hour of contemplative prayer as we sit in the presence of God, with the Holy Spirit, the exposition of the consecrated Host displayed in a starburst monstrance on the altar.

Here's the thing: I have devotional time with God every morning at home. I read the Bible, then a devotional, and I pray. But there is something palpably different going on during Adoration, and there is no other way to say it except that when sitting in the presence of the Blessed Sacrament and allowing my mind to become still, I sense the presence of God in a way that is altogether different than when I pray at home.

"I look at the Master, and the Master looks at me. And the love bounds and abounds." Pope Saint John Paul called it the "wellspring of grace."

During the hour of Adoration, we quiet the mind, empty ourselves, but only so that we can become filled with the Holy Spirit. We do not remain empty, we are joined by God; we form a relationship and an understanding that He is as interested in our concerns as we are.

Weekly Adoration has changed my whole approach to prayer. It has taught me the value of spending an extended time in silent prayerful conversation with God. The hour is needed because when we first arrive our head is full of chatter, and we bring that harried state – and the last thing we were dwelling on – right into Adoration with us. For about the first 20 minutes, my Adoration conversation is all about me.

Eventually, around the 30-minute mark, my mind clears, and I finally turn my attention toward God. In prayer, I will sometimes repeat the name of God, or Jesus, or breathe out to the Holy Spirit, as a means of focusing both my attention and intention on God's presence.

When I finally let go, I am able simply to worship.

As Henri Nouwen wrote, "…solitude is the place where God reveals himself as God with us, as the God who is our creator, redeemer, and sanctifier, as the God who is the source, the center and the purpose of our existence, as the God who wants to give himself to us with an unconditional unlimited and unrestrained love…

"In solitude, we meet God. In solitude, we leave behind our many activities, concerns, plans, and projects, and enter into the presence of our loving God. There we see that he alone is God, that God is love."

King Badouin of Belgium remarked that sitting before the Blessed Sacrament was like sitting in the sun; nothing is required of you but to come out of the shade, and you only feel the strength of its effects, later. — Sister Briege McKenna

If you cannot make it to a Catholic church to participate in weekly Adoration, there are two keys to bringing this practice into your own home. Set aside one hour where you can sit in silence, undisturbed. This allows for the quieting of the mental chatter which is so necessary to get past. Second, to bring your mind into God's presence, it is helpful to read a passage or two from the Bible before you begin. For this the Psalms are particularly helpful. But most of all, we need to be willing to sit in the stillness of the presence of God.

Ironically, it is when we are finally silent that we realize we are not alone: "God's Spirit is right alongside helping us along. If we don't know how or what to pray, it doesn't matter. He does our praying in and for us, making prayer out of our wordless sighs, our aching groans. He knows us far better than we know ourselves, knows our pregnant condition, and keeps us present before God."

WEEK THREE

Why should we live lives that allow people
to see Jesus Christ in us?

DAY 14

[16-20] Because of this decision we don't evaluate people by what they have or how they look. We looked at the Messiah that way once and got it all wrong, as you know. We certainly don't look at him that way anymore. Now we look inside, and what we see is that anyone united with the Messiah gets a fresh start, is created new. The old life is gone; a new life burgeons! Look at it! All this comes from the God who settled the relationship between us and him, and then called us to settle our relationships with each other. God put the world square with himself through the Messiah, giving the world a fresh start by offering forgiveness of sins. God has given us the task of telling everyone what he is doing. We're Christ's representatives. God uses us to persuade men and women to drop their differences and enter into God's work of making things right between them. We're speaking for Christ himself now: Become friends with God; he's already a friend with you.

2 Corinthians 5:16-20 (MSG)

On Tuesday evening while a gentle snow fell, twenty volunteers gathered in the small kitchen and community room of Saint John's Episcopal Church. They set out slow cookers containing soup, set up tables, covered them with red gingham, filled baskets with fresh bread, fruit, cookies, and cakes.

By the end of the evening, two hundred meals would be provided to appreciative young men and women, most of them employees of the ski resort, living on a budget. In a corner of the dining area, Teresa was finishing up the last of the Thanksgiving grocery bags which would provide 400 families throughout Summit County with a Thanksgiving meal this year.

On Tuesday night, volunteers served bowls of soup, cleared tables, and made ready for the next group of young people who sat in pews in the church sanctuary, patiently waiting their turn at one of fifty seats at the table.

My place was at the kitchen sink next to MJ. She patiently dried while I clumsily tried to figure out the quickest system to wash silverware for the next round of kids. We talked as we worked. I'd only met MJ that evening, but she knew me because of my columns. She asked about my mother, and nodded when I shared a bit of news, and I had the impression she already knew me well. I felt blessed to have met such a lovely new friend.

Three hours later, when tables and chairs and tablecloths were folded and put away, we were all tired but happy.

When Pat and Verne dropped me home at the base of my steep driveway, I kissed Pat on the cheek and said, "Thank you. I've been having my dark days again, but I feel better now."

When we allow ourselves to become the hands, feet, eyes, ears, and mouth of Jesus, we can let others see Jesus not only in us, but understand Jesus real presence in the world.

As we serve others, we continue to perform Jesus' miraculous feeding of five thousand. As we dedicate our time and talent to endeavors that help and heal, the medical research we produce heals the sick, the houses we build provide shelter for the homeless.

When Jesus is alive in us and working through us, we make the world better, one person and neighborhood at a time. But first, we must open our hearts to Jesus, to invite him into our lives, and ask him to work in us, to help us become the good people who can do good work in this world.

DAY 15

[30-33] "If God gives such attention to the appearance of wildflowers—most of which are never even seen—don't you think he'll attend to you, take pride in you, do his best for you? What I'm trying to do here is to get you to relax, to not be so preoccupied with getting, so you can respond to God's giving. People who don't know God and the way he works fuss over these things, but you know both God and how he works. Steep your life in God-reality, God-initiative, God-provisions. Don't worry about missing out. You'll find all your everyday human concerns will be met.

[34] "Give your entire attention to what God is doing right now, and don't get worked up about what may or may not happen tomorrow. God will help you deal with whatever hard things come up when the time comes.

Matthew 6:31-34 (MSG)

Morning walks with my Newfoundland dogs are an experience of vibrant colors so stark that they stand against one another, sharp delineated lines that can only be found in nature as she heralds her last glory before the dormancy of winter. Quandary Peak cuts the cloudless sky with sharp-edged steel colored rock among the first blankets of winter snow, sinking into pine green forests and golden Aspens, as my eye travels down the mountain's flank to the dirt road where I stand.

The view reminds me of an insight from a book I read during the autumn's opposite, something I picked up last spring when I had pneumonia. The Lily of the Field and the Bird of the Air, by 19th-century theologian and philosopher Soren Kierkegaard, is a 51-page treatise on 10 verses from the sixth chapter of Matthew.

The Scripture takes up our response to God's providence:

"So, do not worry, saying, 'What shall we eat?' or 'What shall we drink?' or 'What shall we wear?'… your heavenly Father knows that you need them. But seek first his kingdom and his righteousness, and all these things will be given to you as well."

What does it mean to seek first God's kingdom? Seeking seems to require activity, doing. My tendency might be to create a list of activities to demonstrate how eager I am to reach the Kingdom, to please God — as if I could use this as currency to beg for His help with my needs.

Counterintuitively, Kierkegaard instructs us that first we must stop. Stop doing. Stop striving and become silent. Our silence and inaction enable us to turn our complete attention to God, and thereby seek God's perfect plan before we begin constructing our own.

Only when our hearts and minds quiet enough to hear God's thoughts is God truly our priority. Our readiness to stop and listen for God's instruction is our strength. In wordless surrender, we finally acknowledge that God is our Source for everything we need, he knows our needs, and He will provide perfectly.

When I go out for a morning walk with my dogs and my mind is filled with worry and plans of what I must accomplish today, I fail to notice the colors of nature. I miss the birdsong. And most certainly, I miss the "still, small voice of God."

Only when I quiet my mind can I be present to experience the beauty of my surroundings, to acknowledge that in this moment all is well, and in the silence, I can experience God's assurance. As we pursue silent communion with God in the midst our worries, we demonstrate our trust in God's goodness.

As we trust God that our needs are met, we open our hearts and our hands to give others the help they need. We have God's assurance that there is more than enough for everyone. We serve a limitless God.

DAY 16

¹⁻² When Jesus saw his ministry drawing huge crowds, he climbed a hillside. Those who were apprenticed to him, the committed, climbed with him. Arriving at a quiet place, he sat down and taught his climbing companions. This is what he said:

³ "You're blessed when you're at the end of your rope. With less of you there is more of God and his rule.

⁴ "You're blessed when you feel you've lost what is most dear to you. Only then can you be embraced by the One most dear to you.

⁵ "You're blessed when you're content with just who you are—no more, no less. That's the moment you find yourselves proud owners of everything that can't be bought.

⁶ "You're blessed when you've worked up a good appetite for God. He's food and drink in the best meal you'll ever eat.

⁷ "You're blessed when you care. At the moment of being 'care-full,' you find yourselves cared for.

⁸ "You're blessed when you get your inside world—your mind and heart—put right. Then you can see God in the outside world.

⁹ "You're blessed when you can show people how to cooperate instead of compete or fight. That's when you discover who you really are, and your place in God's family.

[10] "You're blessed when your commitment to God provokes persecution. The persecution drives you even deeper into God's kingdom. Matthew 5:1-10 (MSG)

For most of us, our walk of faith exists within the walls of a church. But others find themselves drawn to walk out their faith in the world.

I meant to begin this column last night, but other commitments got in the way. And so when I went to bed and fell asleep, I discovered that my dutiful mind began to write it without me.

Around 3:30 a.m. I woke from a fascinating dream conveying the opening sentence of this column. Unfortunately, I was too tired to get out of bed and write down what I'd seen, so I reminded myself to think of it again in the morning. Incredibly I did remember it, and I'll share it with you. But first I want to tell you what inspired the dream.

On a recent Saturday morning, I met Maggie Ducayet for coffee at The Crown on Main Street in Breckenridge, Colorado. Maggie is a remarkable woman, one of those people with a unique talent for organizing and getting people involved in her good works.

On this recent Saturday morning, we met to talk about a foundation she helped to found fifteen years ago, Summit in Honduras. Their tag-line says it all: "Making a difference in the lives of children and families in rural Honduras."

Summit in Honduras is a small organization that leverages its impact exponentially by partnering with other humanitarian agencies such as Rotary chapters of Summit County and Santa Barbara, Potters for Peace, and Serving at the Crossroads, to provide medical supplies, build and equip schools, fund micro-enterprises, and provide mechanisms for clean water.

Over our Saturday morning coffee, Maggie described a lifetime of pursuing God, with her faith blossoming into a passion for helping others, working with underprivileged youth first in Chicago, then Houston, and now in Honduras.

Walking my faith is often an internal journey of reading and thinking and praying to know better what it means to have a relationship with God, and reporting back what I discover.

For Maggie, walking her faith means taking her love for God and walking it out into the world. There she gives God's love to others. This attitude seems entirely in line with the life of Jesus Christ. Did he teach in grand temples exclusive to the wealthy and scholarly? No. Jesus went out into the world and never turned away from our poverty and imperfection.

On dusty roads, he healed a woman who only dared to touch the hem of his robe. By a stream, he healed a man blind from birth. In a field, he fed 5,000 hungry souls who didn't have enough to eat, and then he filled their hearts with a love that endured forever.

Jesus would never have reached so many people if he had remained within the walls of a temple. By living his ministry in the world, he demonstrated that his saving message of love is for everyone. And he wants us to follow his example.

Around a dinner table, he drank wine, broke bread and gave us not only a way to remember him, but in our communion, he shows us that we are all fed and loved equally by God.

As for my strange dream? It went like this: It was night, and I was walking beside a towering wall of marble grasping a wooden railing. Just in front of me, a dense forest of towering blue spruce stood, separated from me by a narrow strip of well-manicured lawn.

I saw a woman walk into the woods, and I wondered if she would get lost. And then a voice inside of me said, "No, look closely." When I did, I saw a beam of light streaming from her heart, lighting her way through the dark woods. And the voice said, "That Light, the Light of Jesus Christ, will light her way."

DAY 17

¹⁻² On your feet now—applaud God!
   Bring a gift of laughter,
   sing yourselves into his presence.
³ Know this: God is God, and God, God.
   He made us; we didn't make him.
   We're his people, his well-tended sheep.
⁴ Enter with the password: "Thank you!"
   Make yourselves at home, talking praise.
   Thank him. Worship him.
⁵ For God is sheer beauty,
   all-generous in love,
   loyal always and ever.
Psalm 100:1-5 (MSG)

I arrived at Mass an hour early. It was my first time as a Lector (reader), and I wanted to make sure that I did it right. I went to the lectern, and read the Old Testament and New Testament readings that had been assigned to the Mass that evening. I'd been practicing all week, but I knew I would be nervous standing before the congregation for the first time.

Despite my introversion, I love God's Word and enjoy sharing its beauty with others. As I was to learn, there is something special about reading it aloud during Mass. I ran through both passages twice. Then I went and sat in the pew assigned to readers, to wait for Mass to begin.

And here's what I saw…

For the next forty-five minutes, familiar faces scurried around the church preparing for Mass. Barb Rasmussen lighted candles and prepared the altar. Later, she would take her place at the front door with Margie Breslin to greet parishioners. Steve, our Cantor, and Maggie, our pianist, were in the chapel warming up to lead the congregation in song.

Deacon Chuck read through the list of prayer requests, and while the church buzzed with preparations, Father Joe was hearing confessions in the confessional at the back of the church.

Fifteen minutes before Mass started, four men and women who would serve as Eucharistic Ministers picked up the wooden cross necklace that they would wear as they served the consecrated bread and wine later in the Mass. And then it was time to begin.

I completed my first reading, sat down on the bench behind the lectern while Steve took my place to lead us in singing Psalm 40. Steve sung the opening verse: "I have waited, waited for the Lord, and he stooped toward me." The congregation sang the response: "Lord, come to my aid!"

When I heard the Psalm's words and meaning come to life as it was sung, tears came to my eyes with the stark difference between reading the psalm silently at home and hearing it sung in this sacred setting.

I understood two things in that moment: why the Psalms are meant to be sung, and why we take care to prepare ourselves to deliver our part of the Mass. As Steve finished and I rose to read a passage from Hebrews, I asked God to help me to convey the beauty of His Word as well.

On a bright Sunday morning two blocks away at Father Dyer's United Methodist Church, Taylor Katherine and Charlie Moorefield ring the church bell to welcome everyone to church. Barb Cole coordinates the volunteers who read the week's Bible reading, call the congregation to light candles for prayer intentions, and welcome visitors with complimentary tubes of lip balm, a mountain necessity. Then there are the beautiful voices of the volunteer choir led by Music Director, Jason Wilber, and Accompanist, Steve Worrall.

Even at Saint Dunstan's small storefront church, made up of eight to ten ardent believers who began their church in a member's home. The Sunday Mass is led by the Reverend John Longcamp, a retired pediatrician, who followed a calling to become ordained and establish a church that follows a traditional Anglican liturgy. Ken Mace, a retired architect, assists as a server, and Bonnie Schmidt plays traditional hymns on the organ.

Last Saturday evening as I sat waiting for Mass to begin, I realized what I had missed in previous weeks when I showed up ten minutes before church started: how vital volunteers are to the life of each of our churches.

When we notice these people, who greet us each week, collect the offering, sing in the choir, if we think of them at all, we might surmise that they have a special calling or gift, and we have neither the time nor talent to join them.

Not at all. All that is required is to show up thirty-minutes early once or twice a month. Every church needs the participation of more members of its congregation. Far too often, a few faithful souls are carrying more than their share of the volunteer load.
Let's change that.

DAY 18

6-7 While they were there, the time came for her to give birth. She gave birth to a son, her firstborn. She wrapped him in a blanket and laid him in a manger, because there was no room in the hostel.

An Event for Everyone

8-12 There were sheepherders camping in the neighborhood. They had set night watches over their sheep. Suddenly, God's angel stood among them and God's glory blazed around them. They were terrified. The angel said, "Don't be afraid. I'm here to announce a great and joyful event that is meant for everybody, worldwide: A Savior has just been born in David's town, a Savior who is Messiah and Master. This is what you're to look for: a baby wrapped in a blanket and lying in a manger."

13-14 At once the angel was joined by a huge angelic choir singing God's praises:

Glory to God in the heavenly heights,
Peace to all men and women on earth who please him.

15-18 As the angel choir withdrew into heaven, the sheepherders talked it over. "Let's get over to Bethlehem as fast as we can and see for ourselves what God has revealed to us." They left, running, and found Mary and Joseph, and the baby lying in the manger. Seeing was believing. They told everyone they met what the angels had said about this child. All who heard the sheepherders were impressed.

¹⁹⁻²⁰ Mary kept all these things to herself, holding them dear, deep within herself. The sheepherders returned and let loose, glorifying and praising God for everything they had heard and seen. It turned out exactly the way they'd been told!

Luke 2:6-20 (MSG)

Over the past twenty years, I've lived in Baku, Azerbaijan, Kiev, Ukraine, in Tahoe, Fort Lauderdale, Whitefish, Evergreen and now, Breckenridge. In each location, the first place I sought out was the local Catholic church.

I looked forward to attending Mass knowing I would immediately feel at home as I experienced the familiar beauty of Communion. Whether I felt welcome could be determined by a warm greeting. If you've been a member of your neighborhood church for decades, you might doubt the impact you can have.

But imagine for a moment that you are standing in front of the manger. Notice Saint Joseph kneeling next to his beloved wife. Then follow his gaze to Mary holding our Savior, who on this cold winter night is just a baby. She looks lovingly at this precious child she knows is destined to save the world.

And then she looks at you. Her eyes ask the question: "Will you open your heart to help my Son? Will you welcome the stranger sitting next to you so they can discover the love and joy that you have found in Jesus' Church?"

On a dark and snowy Christmas Eve in Evergreen, Colorado. My 85-year-old mother and I had just moved from Florida. We were very excited to join the community but we didn't know a single person. When we arrived at Christ the King Church for Mass we were not only late, we'd entered through the side entrance, right next to the altar, just as the priest was reading the gospel.

The church was packed to the choir loft rafters. We hurriedly slid into the nearest pew, still spinning with unfamiliarity and embarrassment at being late. After the homily, the man sitting next to us smiled and said hello. I explained that we were new, and he responded by welcoming Mom and I and assuring us that we would love our new church, that it was filled with newcomers and long-time residents. And then he wished us a very merry Christmas.

One simple conversation that occurred seven years ago. I don't remember the man's name, only how welcome he made us feel on that wintery night. During this Advent and Christmas, our churches will be crowded with unfamiliar faces, some will be on holiday from other states, others live a few streets away.

You've spent the day shopping in crowded malls and battling crowded highways to get to church, so the last thing you want to see is a stranger sitting in your favorite pew. You might even be tempted to grumble as you slide in next to them.

The crowded churches we face at Christmas feel like a nuisance. But I believe they are filled with people who have been called by Jesus Christ, Himself! They might not know it was Jesus, only they felt a faint tugging on their heart, on their sleeve by a child, or nagged into going by a spouse or parent.

Don't be fooled by their sullen gaze. They have been called to witness and celebrate the birth of Jesus, by no less than God, who is gently reaching out to them. They might come once a year, but this annual visit is fueled by a desire to meet Jesus, not only in the Eucharist but in each of us.

But as one of those strangers, might I ask you a favor?

Say hello to me. Welcome me to church, ask my name, shake my hand, and at the end of service tell me you hope you'll see me next week. If you're feeling festive, invite me to join you and the other parishioners for coffee and donuts in the church kitchen.

That's what happened in the church I now call home. Barb is the quintessential grandma, with a smile that brightens the heart of everyone she encounters as one of the greeters at St. Mary's in Breckenridge.

When I began attending Mass at St. Mary's, I would slip in and out of church without saying a word. Finally, Barb stopped me, said hello, introduced herself and gave me a hug of welcome. Every week after that she did the same.

Because of Barb, I felt welcome in my new church. I lingered after Mass to meet other parishioners, began attending Adoration on Thursday's, and recently I become a Lector.

One person can make all the difference. The smile we share, our warm greeting, might be the only one they receive that day. When we greet a stranger during Mass, we become the hands and heart of Jesus welcoming his beloved to His Church.

Jesus asks us to use this Christmas to share our love for Him and for our church and faith. He's done hard part, bringing them to church. All Jesus asks of us, is that we share the love He shared with us when we were strangers.

DAY 19

²⁶⁻²⁸ In the sixth month of Elizabeth's pregnancy, God sent the angel Gabriel to the Galilean village of Nazareth to a virgin engaged to be married to a man descended from David. His name was Joseph, and the virgin's name, Mary. Upon entering, Gabriel greeted her:

Good morning!
You're beautiful with God's beauty,
Beautiful inside and out!
God be with you.

²⁹⁻³³ She was thoroughly shaken, wondering what was behind a greeting like that. But the angel assured her, "Mary, you have nothing to fear. God has a surprise for you: You will become pregnant and give birth to a son and call his name Jesus.

He will be great,
   be called 'Son of the Highest.'
The Lord God will give him
   the throne of his father David;
He will rule Jacob's house forever—
   no end, ever, to his kingdom."

³⁴ Mary said to the angel, "But how? I've never slept with a man."

³⁵ The angel answered,

The Holy Spirit will come upon you,
   the power of the Highest hover over you;
Therefore, the child you bring to birth
   will be called Holy, Son of God.

36-38 "And did you know that your cousin Elizabeth conceived a son, old as she is? Everyone called her barren, and here she is six months pregnant! Nothing, you see, is impossible with God."

And Mary said,

Yes, I see it all now:
    I'm the Lord's maid, ready to serve.
Let it be with me
    just as you say.
Then the angel left her.
Luke 1:26-38 (MSG)

1-2 The fundamental fact of existence is that this trust in God, this faith, is the firm foundation under everything that makes life worth living. It's our handle on what we can't see. The act of faith is what distinguished our ancestors, set them above the crowd.
Hebrews 11:1 (MSG)

In Hebrews 11:1 we are told that faith is the evidence of things not seen. When we read this passage of the Annunciation, of Mary being greeted by the Angel Gabriel, we read about Mary's great faith in this moment, her willingness to step into the unknown and say, 'yes' to God's invitation to be part of the greatest miracle in history, an event so great is would literally tear history in two, into before and after.

Mary couldn't have known all of that in that one moment. Nor could she know how she would have her heartbroken as her young thirty-three-year-old son was beaten, or would experience the horror of watching him slowly and painfully die on wooden beams as life slowly ebbs from his lungs.
She didn't know any of that, but still, she said yes.

Certainly, as a young Jewish woman, she would have listened in expectation to stories about the coming of the Messiah. But how in that moment, did she comprehend that she would bear a child who would become the Messiah?

This idea must have seemed at once awe-inspiring and frightening.

Faith? Yes, Mary must have had great faith in God to say yes to so many unknowns.

But I also believe she exhibited great courage. After all, once the angel of the Lord had left her, she would be alone. She would have to face the questions and the possible ridicule and perhaps worse, death, for an inexplicable pregnancy.

Yet, she said yes.

God wisely chose Mary, because he understood her great courage.

What does God ask of us?

I believe God never asks more of any of us than we are capable of. We are never promised that our trials will be easy, but we are promised that God will be with us through each of them, and that we will never be given more than we can handle.

Perhaps when we face times of faith-testing difficulties, we can remember Mary's courage, her willingness to say yes, and follow her example. Even when we, don't see the entire way forward. In those moments, let's say yes to God's plan for our lives and trust that we will be guided and strengthened and ultimately hear God say, "Well done my good and faithful servant."

DAY 20

[18-19] The birth of Jesus took place like this. His mother, Mary, was engaged to be married to Joseph. Before they came to the marriage bed, Joseph discovered she was pregnant. (It was by the Holy Spirit, but he didn't know that.) Joseph, chagrined but noble, determined to take care of things quietly so Mary would not be disgraced.

[20-23] While he was trying to figure a way out, he had a dream. God's angel spoke in the dream: "Joseph, son of David, don't hesitate to get married. Mary's pregnancy is Spirit-conceived. God's Holy Spirit has made her pregnant. She will bring a son to birth, and when she does, you, Joseph, will name him Jesus— 'God saves'— because he will save his people from their sins."

Matthew 1:18-23 (MSG)

One year ago, right before Christmas, Mom made a bold move.
We'd lived together for over twenty years after my father passed away. During that time, we'd worked overseas in Kiev, Ukraine; Baku, Azerbaijan, salaried on the Masai Mara in Kenya, and toured the pyramids of Egypt, before finally settling in a nice log home in Evergreen, Colorado.

Mom loved our house in Evergreen, watching the setting sun from her bedroom window or the chickadees that would nest in the birdhouse in a pine tree. She was an active volunteer at the local thrift store, and made friends wherever she went. But on an evening in late November, Mom announced that she was moving back to her condo in Florida.

"Suzie, I went from living with my mother, to living with my husband, to living with you.
I always dreamed of living on my own, and I realize that this is my last chance."
At the age of 88, this was a bold move. But my mother has made courageous choices her entire life.

To be honest, this transition was more difficult for me than it was for Mom.
I'd assumed that we'd live together for the rest of our lives. At which point I would collapse into a puddle of helplessness.

But Mom knew what was best for both of us. Now, I can fully appreciate how wise and generous my mother's decision was. Mom has flourished in Florida, re-establishing ties with her church, her friends, and yes, enjoying her independence. Her move allowed me to come to Breckenridge and discover a place that I love and want to call home. My writing career has thrived and I'm re-establishing an identity and life apart from my mother.

 It would have been easier for Mom to continue to live with me in Colorado. But her decision is an example of the complex wisdom and selfless choices that our mothers and wives make throughout their lives.

My mother never finished high-school because she went to work as a maid in a house down the street to help her widowed mother make ends meet. Yet, Adeline Anderson eventually went to Bible college, and then to work in Juneau, Alaska at a children's orphanage.

After she married my father and moved to Florida, she began working as a teacher. She soon realized that teaching children was her passion, went back to college and received another Bachelors, two Masters, and a Doctorate in Education Administration by going to university at night and on weekends, after working all week. This enabled her to not only have greater skills to serve children, but also to take on positions of greater responsibility, which provided our family with a higher income.

Yet, as a kid, I complained that she wasn't a traditional mother putting dinner on the table each night, or keeping a perfectly tidy home that was decorated to Martha Stewart standards, for every holiday.

Earlier this week, I was talking to Mom about this article and she said that sometimes she wished she hadn't tried so hard to achieve so much, that she should have stayed home to take care of us.

I was shocked and saddened when I heard this. My mother touched the lives of so many children, both in the U.S. and overseas, during her more than fifty years in education. Imagine all the lives that would have lost out on her love and knowledge.

"Mom" is such a weighted term that we forget that behind it is a beautiful woman doing her best. Some women have children and some do not. Some have adopted or fostered or acted as mentors to children in their communities. In one capacity or another, every woman exhibits the qualities of motherhood at some point in her life. I think of Mother Theresa, Saint Elizabeth, Ann Seton, or women in our local community who have, as teachers or nurses or doctors, cared for children with the same tenderness as they would their own.

No matter what your age or hers, it's never too late to honor your mother with thanks. If your mother is no longer alive, send a prayer heavenward, and then appreciate the others in your life: Your wife, your sister, all the women who have made your life better as a result of their wisdom and caring.

A mother's love is demonstrated in small acts every day. Next to the Holy Trinity of God the Father, Jesus the Son, and the Holy Ghost, it is Mary, the Mother of Jesus, who is revered for her open-hearted surrender to God.

For mothers everywhere, Mary is a model of courage, the strong woman who loves unconditionally. As Jesus suffered on the cross, he told his most beloved disciple: 'Behold your Mother'.

I believe this is an instruction for the reverence which we should continue to give Mary, as well as the love and respect we should give our own mothers.

WEEK FOUR

Why do we still need Jesus
in our world today?

DAY 21

⁴⁶⁻⁵⁵ And Mary said,

I'm bursting with God-news;
   I'm dancing the song of my Savior God.
God took one good look at me, and look what
happened—
   I'm the most fortunate woman on earth!
What God has done for me will never be forgotten,
   the God whose very name is holy, set apart from all
others.
His mercy flows in wave after wave
   on those who are in awe before him.
He bared his arm and showed his strength,
   scattered the bluffing braggarts.
He knocked tyrants off their high horses,
   pulled victims out of the mud.
The starving poor sat down to a banquet;
   the callous rich were left out in the cold.
He embraced his chosen child, Israel;
   he remembered and piled on the mercies, piled them
high.
It's exactly what he promised,
   beginning with Abraham and right up to now.

⁵⁶ Mary stayed with Elizabeth for three months and then
went back to her own home. Luke 1:46-55 (MSG)

For you created my inmost being;
    you knit me together in my mother's womb.
[14] I praise you because I am fearfully and wonderfully made;
    your works are wonderful,
    I know that full well.
[15] My frame was not hidden from you
    when I was made in the secret place,
    when I was woven together in the depths of the earth.
[16] Your eyes saw my unformed body;
    all the days ordained for me were written in your book
    before one of them came to be.
[17] How precious to me are your thoughts,[a] God!
    How vast is the sum of them!
[18] Were I to count them,
    they would outnumber the grains of sand—
    when I awake, I am still with you.

Psalm 139:14-18 (NIV)

When we have accepted God's purpose for our lives, there is a sense of right-ness. I remember when I finally realized that my purpose in life was to be a faith writer. One day, many months later, it occurred to me that there is nothing else I could do with my life that would feel this right. This was it.

I had spent years searching for my purpose, my right career, the things I was meant to do with whatever gifts and talents God had given me. Because I believe very strongly that God has given us each a unique purpose in this life, a mission that is meant just for us, that no one else can do quite as well as we can, because it is a purpose sent from Heaven. Created for us by our Creator. And because I'm a bit imaginative, I believe that our souls are restless until we finally discover our purpose, as Saint Augustine said, "our souls are restless until they rest in God".

And so, when I realized my purpose as a faith writer, I felt a sense of contentment and purpose that made me eager to get to work at my computer each day. I dreamt of living to be one hundred and five because I figured it would take that long for me to write everything I wanted to write, to read every book, and to share everything I learned, all for the glory of God.

I'll share a secret with you. When I write, I write for an audience of One. I write for God. Because I love him so.

But I also believe discovering the thing we are meant to do is not just for me, it is for each of us. It is different for each person. For my mother, it was helping children to learn. For someone else it might be building a business that allows them to fund missionary work, or becoming a scientist whose research will save lives. All work is sacred when we do it for the glory of God.

This is why the life and message of Jesus is as necessary to us today was it was over two thousand years ago. And it is why I understand Mary when she says, "My soul magnifies the Lord". Her entire being is bursting with joy because she is fully living God's purpose for her life.

Centuries before self-help books told us we needed to have a purpose in life to be happy, God described what it meant to live a life full of focus and meaning. He knew us before we were born. He created each of us with something special in mind. Something we can accomplish only because it is our God-given purpose.

Some of us discover our purpose early in life. Others, like me, discover it after the age of fifty. No matter. God will use all of our life experiences for His Glory. As we pursue God's plan for our lives, I hope we, following Mary's example, will magnify the Lord, giving thanks to God for our life and our reason for living.

Turn to me and be gracious to me,
    for I am lonely and afflicted.
[17] Relieve the troubles of my heart
    and free me from my anguish.
[18] Look on my affliction and my distress
    and take away all my sins.
[19] See how numerous are my enemies
    and how fiercely they hate me!
[20] Guard my life and rescue me;
    do not let me be put to shame,
    for I take refuge in you.
[21] May integrity and uprightness protect me,
    because my hope, Lord,[c] is in you.

Psalm 25:16-21 (NIV)

In grade school, I was a troublemaker. When our math teacher warned that the next person who spoke would be kicked out of the test, I was compelled to ask if he meant 'now'.

During French class, sounding like a crazed Julia Child, I asked loudly and repeatedly, "Ou est le salle de bain?" Although surely, I knew the bathroom was across the hall. I excelled at making my classmates laugh. Which might lead you to believe that I was beloved by all.

Nothing was further from the truth. I was so lonely that I joined the swim team so I could earn the right to sit at the popular kids table during lunch. Although I became a state swimming champion and received an athletic scholarship to the University of Michigan, I never made it to the popular table.

Even now, so many years later, people often confuse my ready smile with ease and extroversion. But my closest friends recognize when I've retreated into my house for too long and need to be called back into the world.

Turn to me and be gracious to me, for I am lonely and afflicted. (Psalm 25:16)

Loneliness is insidious and invisible to the casual observer. I take it for granted in my own life, but recently I was surprised to find it surface in friends who I assumed were surrounded and nourished by loved ones. But that's the mask of loneliness.

It hides behind busy-ness. Your lovely friend who volunteers for every committee, the one who is known as a people-connector, or the quiet one who smiles and nods as we sit around a table talking not noticing her silence. Being lonely has nothing to do with being alone.

It is all too often that after an evening spent with friends, I come home and realize that the blue dog of loneliness has slipped into the house behind me and is now curled at my feet as I turn on the TV and pick up my knitting. Or at the end of a meal, just as companionable conversation begins to approach real intimacy, we glance at our watches, pay the check, and reach for our coats.

We don't do it on purpose. We don't notice the nudge of need, except for that closing of our throats as we try to tell someone how we're doing. But we stop ourselves, embarrassed at the burden of our vulnerability. We are in the company of friends so how could we feel lonely?

But recall, on the night before he was crucified, Jesus went up the mountain to pray. He knew what he faced and so he asked his disciples, his closest friends, to wait with him, to keep him company on his last night on Earth, on the last night before he would suffer unspeakable pain and degradation.

He was only gone an hour, not more, just a short time to pray and ask his father if this cup of suffering could be taken away. He knew the answer, of course it could not. He returned to his friends and found them asleep. Alone and heartbroken. Jesus understood he would face the darkness alone.

(And therefore, you must share your loneliness with Jesus. He understands your desolation and despair. His heart will hold your pain and replace it with love.)

Companionship is when we share a meal, a walk through snowy woods, a movie.

Intimacy is manna from heaven created for souls to find in each other and in our relationship with God. Which loneliness seeks to devour. It isolates us and tells the lie that we are no longer loved or needed. That the one who died or left us was the only one who could save us. It builds walls around us so that all we hear is the echo of our emptiness.

But loneliness is a paper tiger. Easily, effortlessly destroyed with time and attention. The most effective weapons against loneliness are unremarkable. Looking someone in the eye when they speak to us. Listening without interruption, without hurrying to make a comparison. Giving the gift of undivided attention. Asking how they are doing and waiting for more, after they tell us they are fine.

It's not easy to open our heart to the loneliness of another person because we might unearth our own. We want to skate across the surface of our relationships. And most of the time that is all we need. But we should open our heart to seeing a friend or acquaintance who may on occasion, if only for an hour, need the soul-linking of real conversation.

When we ask why Jesus is still needed in our world, one reason is that his words are as healing today as they were then. When we cannot find someone to listen to us, Jesus will. He is always present, he always surrounds us with his love. We need Jesus every day because his presence heals our broken places.

DAY 23

⁸⁻¹² There were sheepherders camping in the neighborhood. They had set night watches over their sheep. Suddenly, God's angel stood among them and God's glory blazed around them. They were terrified. The angel said, "Don't be afraid. I'm here to announce a great and joyful event that is meant for everybody, worldwide: A Savior has just been born in David's town, a Savior who is Messiah and Master. This is what you're to look for: a baby wrapped in a blanket and lying in a manger."

¹³⁻¹⁴ At once the angel was joined by a huge angelic choir singing God's praises:

Glory to God in the heavenly heights,
Peace to all men and women on earth who please him.
 Luke 2:8-14 (MSG)

It is only fitting that during this season of light, we should encounter angels among us. Pat Hoogheem is my angel.

Despite a long list of Christmas things to be done, she accompanied me to the Good Samaritan hospital in Denver as I went for surgery on the wrist I broke while cross country skiing. She returned home with me, and spent the night on the couch so I wouldn't be alone. But that is only one example of her friendship over the past three years. When I have fallen into the despair of depression, Pat will call and insist I accompany her to our knitting group, or come over for dinner, or anything that will help me to get out of my own head.

I am blessed by Pat's friendship. I hope we all experience this type of friendship at least once in our lives. But this type of unconditional love is only a glimpse of the love that God has for each of us.

What brought me into the Church was Jesus and his message of love freely given. What keeps me in the Church is Jesus' call to a lifelong relationship that grows more meaningful as I discover the endless depths of his love.

When I read the life and the teachings of Jesus Christ, I discover a message of peace, justice, compassion, and caring for each of us, rich and poor, locals and immigrants, old and young. From His humble birth in a manger to an ignoble death on a cross, the King of Kings demonstrated how to live, by becoming one of us.

The birth of Jesus marks a turning point in the history of mankind. For the first time, we encounter a leader who sought not to conquer but to serve, not to amass riches but to feed the poor.

Our God our Savior revealed the miraculous power of love: That he loved us so much he would forgive us anything and in return offer us everything in heaven and a better way to live here on earth.

Jesus' love is for each of us, no matter where we are, what we have done, he embraces us with a simple and enduring message:

"This is My commandment, that you love one another as I loved you. Greater love has no one than this, that he lay down his life for his friends. You are My friends…because everything I have learned from My Father I have made known to you. You did not choose Me, but I chose you. And I appointed you to go and bear fruit— fruit that will remain—so that whatever you ask the Father in My name, He will give you. This is My command to you: Love one another." John 15:12-17 (NIV)

On this darkest winter night, we celebrate a divine spark of light ignited and never extinguished. The moment God's love became Jesus and we discovered that love grows as it is given and shared and like God, because it is from God, can never be diminished.

Jesus' love is freely given to each of us. You can't earn it. Only accept it. Love that fills those places in our hearts we hide from everyone else.

We should strive to live by the example of Jesus' life. But to be transformed by the power of Jesus' love, we must open our hearts and invite him into our lives.

Begin that journey today, find a church nearby. Come in from the cold, join others in Christmas celebration, and experience God's love for you. It is the most powerful force in the world. From God's love springs compassion to help others, hope when we cannot see the way forward, and peace when we need rest.

Through the birth, life, death, and resurrection of Jesus we gain true love. A love to fill our hearts for the rest of our lives, never ending, always growing.

Jesus is love, actually. And he loves you.

DAY 24

Christmas Eve

In those days, a decree went out from Caesar Augustus that the whole world should be enrolled.
This was the first enrollment, when Quirinius was governor of Syria. So, all went to be enrolled, each to his own town.
And Joseph too went up from Galilee from the town of Nazareth to Judea, to the city of David that is called Bethlehem, because he was of the house and family of David, to be enrolled with Mary, his betrothed, who was with child.
While they were there, the time came for her to have her child, and she gave birth to her firstborn son. She wrapped him in swaddling clothes and laid him in a manger, because there was no room for them in the inn.
Luke 2:10-14 (NIV)

We began our Advent journey on a dark night in the beginning of December. Christmas seemed far off at that point. But here we are.

It's another cold dark winter night. But we have come so far. Like the shepherds alone in a field, we have seen a beckoning light, calling us toward Bethlehem.

Tonight, we are called to the humble village, to find a young couple bent over a manger, staring at a helpless infant, newborn.

We feel compelled to kneel with the shepherds. Perhaps we can't describe the reason that causes us to drop to our knees in awe, but we know there has never been another moment like this in history. There never will be again, until of course, Jesus returns.

But here, wrapped in swaddling rags, on a mattress of sweet smelling hay, is our Savior. What can we say to welcome him? The words are caught in our throat.

But overhead, we hear the beginning of a song, which grows louder and then we realize Heaven has opened and the sky is filled with a choir of angels singing, Glory to God in the Highest, and Peace to His People on Earth.

We don't have to say a word, because our souls have joined the heavenly choir and all the stars in the sky glorifying our Newborn King.

DAY 25

Christmas Day

[16-18] "This is how much God loved the world: He gave his Son, his one and only Son. And this is why: so that no one need be destroyed; by believing in him, anyone can have a whole and lasting life. God didn't go to all the trouble of sending his Son merely to point an accusing finger, telling the world how bad it was. He came to help, to put the world right again. Anyone who trusts in him is acquitted; anyone who refuses to trust him has long since been under the death sentence without knowing it. And why? Because of that person's failure to believe in the one-of-a-kind Son of God when introduced to him.

John 3:16-18 (MSG)

[20-21] "Look at me. I stand at the door. I knock. If you hear me call and open the door, I'll come right in and sit down to supper with you.

Revelation 3:20 (MSG)

If you have arrived at Christmas day feeling empty rather than filled with joy, please take this moment to re-read the Bible verses for today, there are two important messages for you:

From the first moment Adam and Eve were created through every moment of every day, to this moment, God has pursued you with a love that is bigger than anything you can imagine.

God loves you so much that he came down from Heaven, took the human form of a vulnerable, precious infant. He grew with us, walked with us, experienced our hurt, our loneliness, our hunger, and our pain.

But he also shared our laughter, our joy, our love.

And in the end, he did the only thing he could do to prove that he loved us so dearly he was willing to bear our sin and sacrifice his life for ours. (John 3:16-18)

Even after, as imperfect history and well-meaning, but misguided teachers and churches drove some of us away, Jesus never gave up on us.

Today, he stands at the door of our heart and knocks. All we have to do is open our hearts and yes. We are loved more than words can describe. Will you say yes?

You are loved so dearly by God.

FROM THIS DAY FORWARD...

[31] "When the Son of Man comes in his glory, and all the angels with him, he will sit on his glorious throne. [32] All the nations will be gathered before him, and he will separate the people one from another as a shepherd separates the sheep from the goats. [33] He will put the sheep on his right and the goats on his left.

[34] "Then the King will say to those on his right, 'Come, you who are blessed by my Father; take your inheritance, the kingdom prepared for you since the creation of the world. [35] For I was hungry and you gave me something to eat, I was thirsty and you gave me something to drink, I was a stranger and you invited me in, [36] I needed clothes and you clothed me, I was sick and you looked after me, I was in prison and you came to visit me.'

[37] "Then the righteous will answer him, 'Lord, when did we see you hungry and feed you, or thirsty and give you something to drink? [38] When did we see you a stranger and invite you in, or needing clothes and clothe you? [39] When did we see you sick or in prison and go to visit you?'

[40] "The King will reply, 'Truly I tell you, whatever you did for one of the least of these brothers and sisters of mine, you did for me.'

[41] "Then he will say to those on his left, 'Depart from me, you who are cursed, into the eternal fire prepared for the devil and his angels. [42] For I was hungry and you gave me nothing to eat, I was thirsty and you gave me nothing to drink, [43] I was a stranger and you did not invite me in, I needed clothes and you did not clothe me, I was sick and in prison and you did not look after me.'

[44] "They also will answer, 'Lord, when did we see you hungry or thirsty or a stranger or needing clothes or sick or in prison, and did not help you?'

[45] "He will reply, 'Truly I tell you, whatever you did not do for one of the least of these, you did not do for me.'

[46] "Then they will go away to eternal punishment, but the righteous to eternal life."

Matthew 25:31-46 (NIV)

We don't often hear sermons about the Second Coming of Jesus. I'm not sure if it's because it's a difficult idea for us to comprehend, or if we feel that we have enough problems getting through this life as good and moral people.

On the last Sunday before Advent, we celebrated the Solemnity of Christ the King. The gospel reading was this passage from the Gospel of Matthew. Father Felician spoke about this gospel reading in such a way, that I finally had the beginnings of what the Second Coming of Jesus would be like and why it would be necessary.

The people looked for a Messiah, hoped for a warrior king, a political leader, who would free them from enslavement by enemies in other countries.

Instead, we received a Messiah who offers us freedom that will endure forever. It is a spiritual freedom, something to save our lives, save our souls. But more than an 'insurance policy' against eternal damnation, this freedom can change our lives and help us to live to the best of our potential.

Here is where I see how we will be measured in the Second Coming:

"When the Son of Man comes in his glory, and all the angels with him, he will sit on his glorious throne. [32] All the nations will be gathered before him, and he will separate the people one from another as a shepherd separates the sheep from the goats. [33] He will put the sheep on his right and the goats on his left.

[34] "Then the King will say to those on his right, 'Come, you who are blessed by my Father; take your inheritance, the kingdom prepared for you since the creation of the world. [35] For I was hungry and you gave me something to eat, I was thirsty and you gave me something to drink, I was a stranger and you invited me in, [36] I needed clothes and you clothed me, I was sick and you looked after me, I was in prison and you came to visit me.'

[37] "Then the righteous will answer him, 'Lord, when did we see you hungry and feed you, or thirsty and give you something to drink? [38] When did we see you a stranger and invite you in, or needing clothes and clothe you? [39] When did we see you sick or in prison and go to visit you?'

[40] "The King will reply, 'Truly I tell you, whatever you did for one of the least of these brothers and sisters of mine, you did for me.'

That's it. We looked for a king who rule over the world, crush other leaders, enslave his enemies. That is not the Kingdom of Jesus Christ.

Instead, the Second Coming of Jesus will be a King who judges us on how we treated the least among us. Because when we are asked to be Jesus to others, to be his hands that comfort the sorrowful, when we are asked to be his eyes who see injustice and don't turn away, when we are asked to be his mouth, who speaks out in defense of those who cannot speak for themselves, we are living as Christ-within us.

But as we can see from this passage, Jesus asks more from us. 'Truly I tell you, whatever you did for one of the least of these brothers and sisters of mine, you did for me.'

If we only saw Christ within ourselves, we might be susceptible to believing we were more holy than the ones we helped. But when Jesus tells us that when we feed the hungry, we are feeding Jesus, we understand that we are only as holy as those we help.

That is exactly what we are asked to do as members of the Kingdom of God.

Imagine how different our lives would feel if we embraced the true freedom that comes through the love of Jesus Christ.

Imagine the freedom we would experience in the new year if instead of writing out a list of New Year's resolutions, we spent time alone with Jesus in prayer, and sought his direction and goals for our life in the next twelve months? Imagine what an amazing year we'd look forward to!

Thank you for joining me. I wish you a Merry Christmas and a Happy New Year.

Please keep in touch at www.suzanneelizabeths.com

P.S. This time of year can be very lonely for many people, me included. I want to share a letter I wrote two years ago after someone in our small mountain community ended his life. I hope in sharing my own story, someone will be helped.

Dear Friend,

One of the members of our idyllic mountain town could bear his pain no longer and chose to end his life.

This tragic event made me think of you, and the pain you have lived with for so many years. I know there have been moments when the endless despair was more than you could endure. You too, have heard a dark whisper that you should end your life, some nights louder than others.

But wait, please. Don't go yet. First, let me share my story.

I live with depression every day; I understand how someone can reach the point of wanting to take their own life. I have had moments when I asked God what the point of living was when the sadness was so great that even my bones ached.

I am writing this to show you what my darkness feels like, so that you know you are not alone. But then, I want to encourage you to embrace life, to know you are loved, and that your life matters.

I hope this helps…

Two years ago, I went to see my doctor after I had a breast lumpectomy. I'd been plagued with relentless hot flashes, insomnia, and frightening mood swings. I had been taking hormone replacements to help, but after that brush with cancer, they were no longer an option.

My doctor asked if I would be willing to take an anti-depressant which had a side-effect of subduing hot flashes. I nodded 'yes', because if I spoke, I would have cried.

I knew I needed this support, but for fifty years, I was too ashamed to ask for help. I was grateful and yet for two years afterwards, if anyone asked what the little pink pill was, I told them it was for hot flashes, not depression.

A stigma still surrounds mental illness. Yet, if I had a broken leg, I'd be first in line at the doctor's office to get a cast. But why, then when my spirit is broken, do I feel as if it's my fault? That I must hide my depression because to admit it to anyone else would label me as defective.

Dear friend, don't be like me. Don't wait to get help. If you are hurting, go see your doctor now. If you are afraid that your desire to end your life is stronger than your will to live…please call the National Suicide Prevention Hot Line: 1-800-273-8255

You are worthwhile, take care of yourself. There are several treatments for depression: medication, talk therapy, cognitive therapy. Each strategy works in its own way. Work with your doctor to find the best path for your health. And keep trying if the first one doesn't work.

Even with all of these strategies, you may still find yourself confronted with periods of depression that come and go for no reason. As I described to my doctor, on the surface my life is happier than it's ever been. But underneath, there is a lake of sadness and sometimes I feel as if I am swimming through its dark depths.

But there is hope. Each day you must resolve to live in the moment, to promise you will take one step forward. To reach out for help.

Repeat these words to yourself each day, several times a day: I am not alone. My life is worth living. I am loved. There is hope. My life matters. God loves me.

Pastor Rick Warren listed Five Truths that anyone living with mental illness should consider. I would like to share those truths with you, as well as my own experience, in hope that you will find comfort.

> **YOU ARE LOVED** – You find this impossible to believe. When you look in the mirror what you see is unlovable. When you look at your life, you only see what has gone wrong. You are surrounded by beauty but as St. Paul said, you see through a glass darkly.
>
> What you cannot see are all the people who love you. You cannot see what they see, your kindness, your sensitive spirit, your one-of-a-kind genius. You deserve to live.
>
> Get out of bed. Go out into the world. It is vital that you don't isolate yourself. I speak with my mother every day. Sometimes we just chat for ten minutes. Sometimes she is the raft that keeps my head above water. Find someone you can speak with every day.

YOU HAVE A PURPOSE – A purpose? When your life has been filled with failure? Yes, my friend, you have work to do.

Fifty-years from today, you will look back on all of your failures with gratitude, because you will understand that they were necessary to peel away the layers of other people's expectations to reveal your true self.

You are a diamond in the rough. But thanks to your courage, you pushed through every painful failure, shameful days of being broke, and certain you'd fallen so far behind you might as well quit. Yet, you persevered. And now, all these years in the future…you will thank God, because you have become the person you were meant to be…because you didn't give up.

YOU BELONG – And yet, you feel so alone, even in the middle of a crowd.
Go out and talk to one other person today, even if it's only to remark on the weather with the person scanning your groceries. See that you are connected to others. You have a voice. You can make someone else smile.

Volunteer! When you are among other people you will understand that your talents are needed in our community. Sign up to serve dinner at your local homeless shelter. Volunteer at the thrift store. Find a charity that shares your beliefs and join them. Share yourself with others and realize that your talents are needed and you make our community better.

YOU HAVE A CHOICE – This is your secret weapon. You have more courage than you realize. Each day you choose to get up, take another step forward, take another breath, look up, and outward. You choose to do all of this despite a spirit and mind that hurt so much. But you are stronger, so you get up.

This is your strength. Each morning is fresh with hope and possibility. The darkness that hounded you will grow weaker, because you grow stronger. And when it comes again, you will be ready. You are tougher today than yesterday. Take another step. Just one. That's enough. Tomorrow you will take another.

YOU ARE NEEDED – You have a purpose here, now, don't leave us before you have finished the full length of your days. God created you with a special talent and purpose that only you can fulfill. We need you here to fight through the darkness, come out the other side, and share what you have learned, to help us as a community. We need your special strength that only comes because of all that you have been through.

Don't go, my friend. Stay here with me, with all of us who love you. Stay and fight the good fight. Your future is brighter than you could ever imagine.

Tonight, go outside and look up at the stars. See how they shine for you?

God has strewn the night sky with this reminder that you are as unique as each of them. Tonight, and each night, you are covered with a blanket of their promise: You are not alone. Each of those stars represents someone who loves you. Someone who needs you here to love them, too.

You are not alone. Right next to you, God is sitting with you, reaching out to you. Jesus says, "Here I am. Take my strength. I have enough for you." He will say that every day for the rest of your life. You are never alone, because He will never leave you. You are loved beyond measure. You are stronger than you know because His strength is your strength.

My friend, you have a purpose and that gives you hope and courage. Stay and embrace the promise of a new day. We love you. Your life has meaning. Even the darkness will serve you, to show you how beautiful the morning can be. We need you here. Stay, please.

With love,
Your Friend Suzanne

May the Lord answer you
When you are in distress;
May the name of the God of
Jacob protect you.
May he send you help from
The sanctuary
And grant you support from Zion.

May he give you the desire of
Your heart.
And make all your plans succeed.
We will shout for joy when
You are victorious
And will lift up our banners
In the name of our God.
May the Lord grant all your
Requests.
Psalm 20: 1-2,4-5

Made in the USA
Middletown, DE
07 December 2017